To:_____

From:_____

Date:_____

Gods Best

FOR YOUR SUCCESS

God's Best for Your Success

Copyright © by Word, Inc. All rights reserved.

Scripture text taken from The Holy Bible, New King James Version. Copyright © 1979, 1980, 1982 by Thomas Nelson, Inc. No part of this publication may be reproduced, stored in a retrieval system, or transmitted in any form or by any means—electronic, mechanical, photocopy, recording, or any other—except for brief quotations in printed reviews, without the prior written permission of the publisher.

Library of Congress Cataloging-in-Publication Data:
God's best for your success
    p.   cm.
ISBN 0-8499-5155-0
1. Christian life—Quotations, maxims, etc. 2. Bible—Quotations.
3. Success—Religious aspects—Christianity.
I. Word Publishing.
BV4513.G63   1995
242—dc20
95-19186
CIP

God's Best
FOR YOUR SUCCESS

WORD PUBLISHING
Dallas • London • Vancouver • Melbourne

$\mathscr{T}$he world measures success
by the size of a your bank account.
God measures success by the
size of your heart.

*One's life does not consist in the abundance
of the things he possesses.*
LUKE 12:15

$\mathcal{T}$he more God trusts us
with, the more accountable we
are for how we use it.

*For everyone to whom much is given, from him
much will be required; and to whom much has been
committed, of him they will ask the more.*
LUKE 12:48

$\mathcal{T}$here could be no greater reward than seeing Jesus smile when all is said and done. His approval is the measure of our success.

❖

Well done, good and faithful servant; you were faithful over a few things, I will make you ruler over many things. Enter into the joy of your lord.
MATTHEW 25:21

$\mathscr{I}$f it is well with your soul,
you have everything that matters. If it
is not, nothing else matters.

■

For what profit is it to a man if he gains the whole
world, and loses his own soul? Or what will a man give
in exchange for his soul?
MATTHEW 16:26

$\mathcal{J}$esus knows human nature.
Wherever our treasure is, our interest
is sure to follow.

But lay up for yourselves treasures in heaven,
where neither moth nor rust destroys and where thieves
do not break in and steal. For where your treasure is,
there your heart will be also.
MATTHEW 6:20-21

$\mathcal{W}$e may appear successful on the outside, but God knows whether we are successful on the inside.

◼

The LORD does not see as man sees;
for man looks at the outward appearance, but the
LORD looks at the heart.
1 SAMUEL 16:7

$\mathcal{W}$hen God's children are
blessed with wealth, they should use
it wisely to bring glory to him.

◼

The blessing of the LORD makes one rich,
and He adds no sorrow with it.
PROVERBS 10:22

$\mathcal{T}$here are no masters in the kingdom
of God, only servants.

*And whoever of you desires to be first
shall be slave of all.*
MARK 10:44

$\mathcal{T}$here can be only one highest
priority in life.

*But seek first the kingdom of God and His righteousness,
and all these things shall be added to you.*
MATTHEW 6:33

$\mathscr{T}$here is no such thing as a
self-made person.

███

I am the vine, you are the branches. He who abides in Me,
and I in him, bears much fruit; for without
Me you can do nothing
JOHN 15:5

*G*od wants us to win
the race of life.

■

*Do you not know that those who run in a
race all run, but one receives the prize? Run in such a
way that you may obtain it.*
1 CORINTHIANS 9:24

$\mathcal{T}$he formula for peace of mind is simple: don't worry about anything—pray about everything.

Be anxious for nothing, but in everything by prayer and supplication, with thanksgiving, let your requests be made known to God; and the peace of God, which surpasses all understanding, will guard your hearts and minds through Christ Jesus.
PHILIPPIANS 4:6, 7

*I*f you control your tongue, you
will master your life.

■

*For we all stumble in many things. If anyone does not
stumble in word, he is a perfect man, able also to
bridle the whole body.*

*A*lways tell the truth, and
you won't have to remember
what you said.

*Therefore, putting away lying, "Let each one of you
speak truth with his neighbor," for we are
members of one another.*
EPHESIANS 4:25

$\mathcal{T}$he world won't be able to squeeze you from the outside if God has changed you from the inside.

And do not be conformed to this world, but be transformed by the renewing of your mind, that you may prove what is that good and acceptable and perfect will of God.
ROMANS 12:2

$\mathcal{A}$ partner with different values
won't just pull you in a different direction;
he or she will pull you down.

■

*Do not be unequally yoked together with
unbelievers. For what fellowship has
righteousness with lawlessness?*
2 CORINTHIANS 6:14

$\mathcal{G}$od can't be your God if
money is your god. At whose altar do
you sacrifice your best energies?

▨

*No one can serve two masters; for either he
will hate the one and love the other, or else he will be loyal
to the one and despise the other. You cannot
serve God and mammon.*

MATTHEW 6:24

*D*on't be halfhearted in
your work. Whether the task is great
or small, do it with all your
strength. Go for it!

◼

Whatever your hand finds to do, do it with your might.
ECCLESIASTES 9:10

*C*elebrate the successes of others as you would have them celebrate yours.

❚

Rejoice with those who rejoice, . . .
ROMANS 12:15

$\mathscr{F}$inancial security exists mainly
in the imagination.

*The rich man's wealth is his strong city,
and like a high wall in his own esteem.*
PROVERBS 18:11

*Y*ou know it is an
honorable deal if you can sign God's
name to the contract.

❖

*And whatever you do in word or deed, do all
in the name of the Lord Jesus, giving thanks to
God the Father through Him.*
COLOSSIANS 3:17

$\mathcal{P}$lanning without seeking
the will of God is presumptuous
and foolish.

*Come now, you who say, "Today or tomorrow
we will go to such and such a city, spend a year there,
buy and sell, and make a profit"; . . . Instead you ought to say,
"If the Lord wills, we shall live and do this or that."*
JAMES 4:13, 15

$\mathcal{T}$he true power of positive
thinking comes from filling your mind
with the things God approves.

*Finally, brethren, whatever things are true, whatever things
are noble, whatever things are just, whatever things are pure,
whatever things are lovely, whatever things are of good report,
if there is any virtue and if there is anything
praiseworthy—meditate on these things.*
PHILIPPIANS 4:8

$\mathcal{S}$elf-denial and self-sacrifice are keys to success in the Christian life—and in every other worthwhile endeavor.

Then said Jesus unto his disciples, "If any man will come after me, let him deny himself, and take up his cross, and follow me."
MATTHEW 16:24

$\mathscr{S}$uccess lies in only one direction:
straight ahead. If you backtrack,
you get sidetracked.

No one, having put his hand to the plow, and looking back,
is fit for the kingdom of God.
LUKE 9:62

*H*s believers, we may be
knocked down, but we will never
be knocked out.

◼

*We are hard-pressed on every side yet not crushed;
we are perplexed, but not in despair; persecuted, but not
forsaken; struck down, but not destroyed.*
2 CORINTHIANS 4:8, 9

We should work as if God were
our employer. He is the One
we want to please.

◼

And whatever you do, do it heartily, as to the
Lord and not to men, knowing that from the Lord you will
receive the reward of the inheritance;
for you serve the Lord Christ.
COLOSSIANS 3:23, 24

$\mathscr{P}$rayerfully consult with as
many trustworthy advisors as possible
before proceeding with your plans.

▪

*Without counsel, plans go awry, but in the
multitude of counselors they are established.*
PROVERBS 15:22

*W*e need to meet with
God daily to recharge our batteries.
Time out is better than burnout.

But those who wait on the LORD shall renew their strength;
they shall mount up with wings like eagles, they shall run
and not be weary, they shall walk and not faint.
ISAIAH 40:31

$\mathcal{L}$ife is short. We need to make it count
by bringing honor to God.

*So teach us to number our days, that we
may gain a heart of wisdom.*
PSALM 90:12

If God grants you good health,
never retire. Instead, seek a new challenge.

Here I am this day, eighty-five years old. As yet I am as
strong this day as on the day that Moses sent me. . . .
Now therefore, give me this mountain.
JOSHUA 14:10, 12

$\mathscr{A}$ healthy realism about
your own abilities should be matched
by an irrepressible optimism about God's.

Not that we are sufficient of ourselves to think
of anything as being from ourselves,
but our sufficiency is from God.
2 CORINTHIANS 3:5

$\mathscr{T}$rue leaders place the needs of
others above their own.

*In lowliness of mind let each esteem others better than
himself. Let each of you look out not only for his own
interests, but also for the interests of others.*
PHILIPPIANS 2:3, 4

$\mathcal{I}$f you are your own benchmark,
how will you improve?

*But they, measuring themselves by
themselves, and comparing themselves among
themselves, are not wise.*

2 CORINTHIANS 10:12

$\mathscr{I}$f you are alive and breathing, if you have food to eat and clothes to wear, then God has met your basic needs.

And having food and clothing, with these we shall be content.
1 TIMOTHY 6:8

*M*an proposes, but God disposes.

A man's heart plans his way, but the
LORD directs his steps.
PROVERBS 16:9

$\mathcal{I}$n the spiritual realm, as
well as in the natural, your return will
be proportional to your investment.

*He who sows sparingly will also reap
sparingly, and he who sows bountiful will
also reap bountiful.*
2 CORINTHIANS 9:6

$\mathcal{S}$uccess requires persistence.
If it is the right thing, never,
never, never give up.

*Let us not grow weary while doing good, for in due
season we shall reap if we do not lose heart.*
GALATIANS 6:9

$\mathscr{I}$t is amazing what can be accomplished once people put their minds—and their backs—into it.

▪

So we built the wall, and the entire wall
was joined together up to half its height, for the people
had a mind to work.

NEHEMIAH 4:6

*H*eaven has all the
resources, and God has all the power.
What more do we need to succeed?

*And my God shall supply all your need according
to His riches in glory by Christ Jesus.*
PHILIPPIANS 4:19

The children of God
should never be lazy. They should be
enthusiastic, diligent workers.

Not lagging in diligence, fervent in spirit,
serving the Lord; . . .
ROMANS 12:11

*J*esus wants us to have
the richest, fullest life we
could ever imagine.

*I have come that they may have life, and that
they may have it more abundantly.*
JOHN 10:10

$\mathcal{S}$heer ability is not
enough to succeed in life, at least not
for the long haul. Personal integrity
is basic to long-term success.

*So he shepherded them according to the integrity of
his heart, and guided them by the
skillfulness of his hands.*
PSALM 78:72

$\mathcal{I}$f you have thought and
prayed carefully, go ahead and make
your proposal. If God is in it, you may
receive exactly what you ask for.

■

And I said to the king, "If it pleases the king . . .
send me to Judah, to the city of my fathers' tombs,
that I may rebuild it." And the king granted them to me
according to the good hand of my God upon me.
NEHEMIAH 2:5, 8

$\mathcal{O}$ur God is the highest
standard of excellence.

*O LORD, our LORD, how excellent is Your name
in all the earth, who have set Your glory above the heavens!*
PSALM 8:1

*N*othing gladdens
God's heart—or an employer's
heart—more than a willing worker.

Also I heard the voice of the LORD, saying:
"Whom shall I send, and who will go for Us?"
Then I said, "Here am I! Send me."
ISAIAH 6:8

*I*f you shoot at nothing,
you will surely hit it. A successful
person is always goal-oriented.

◾

*Forgetting those things which are behind and reaching
forward to those things which are ahead, I press toward
the goal for the prize of the upward
call of God in Christ Jesus.*
PHILIPPIANS 3:13, 14

$\mathcal{P}$eople were impressed by
the quality of Jesus' life and work. Our
lives should have the same impact.

*And they were astonished beyond measure,
saying, "He has done all things well."*
MARK 7:37

$\mathscr{S}$ome problems require
creative solutions. Use your God-given
imagination and let the ideas flow.

And when they could not come near Him
because of the crowd, they uncovered the roof where He was.
So when they had broken through, they let down the
bed on which the paralytic was lying.

MARK 2:4

$\mathcal{J}$esus was clearly focused on what He was about to do. Nothing worthwhile is accomplished without concentration.

When the time had come for Him to be received up, . . . He steadfastly set His face to go to Jerusalem.
LUKE 9:51

*B*reathe a prayer to God before
you do any business.

Then the king said to me, "What do you request?"
So I prayed to the God of heaven.
NEHEMIAH 2:4

$\mathscr{I}$f you want to win,
play by God's rules.

*And also if anyone competes in athletics,
he is not crowned unless he competes
according to the rules.*
2 TIMOTHY 2:5

$\mathcal{T}$rouble is only temporary.
The lessons it teaches are permanent.

*For our light affliction, which is but for a moment,
is working for us a far more exceeding
and eternal weight of glory.*
2 CORINTHIANS 4:17

$\mathcal{O}$ut of struggle
comes strength of character.

But may the God of all grace, . . .
after you have suffered a while, perfect,
establish, strengthen, and settle you.
1 PETER 5:10

$\mathscr{S}$uccessful people are
self-starters. They are internally
motivated and work hard even if no one
is looking over their shoulder.

◼

Not with eye service, as men-pleasers,
but as bondservants of Christ, doing the
will of God from the heart.
EPHESIANS 6:6

$\mathscr{W}$hen you give to charity,
do it privately. Some day God will
reward you publicly.

*Take heed that you do not do your charitable
deeds before men, to be seen by them. Otherwise you have
no reward from your Father in heaven.*
MATTHEW 6:1

$\mathscr{I}$f you want to live long,
don't try to do everything yourself.

Both you and these people who are with you will
surely wear yourselves out. For this thing is too much for you;
you are not able to perform it by yourself.
EXODUS 18:18

Status seekers work for
perks and strokes. Believers work for
the glory of God.

■

*Beware of the scribes, who desire to go around
in long robes, love greetings in the marketplaces, the best
seats in the synagogues, and the best places at feasts.*
MARK 12:38, 39

$\mathcal{D}$evelop the life of
someone who can carry on your work.

But command Joshua, and encourage him
and strengthen him; for he shall go over before this people.
DEUTERONOMY 3:28

*Y*ou can't take it with you.
Invest what you have in kingdom
business—and collect eternal dividends.

For we brought nothing into this world,
and it is certain we can carry nothing out.
1 TIMOTHY 6:7

*J*esus enveloped his most
important decisions with prayer.
So should we.

*He went out to the mountain to pray, and
continued all night in prayer to God. And when it was day,
He called His disciples to Himself; and from them He
chose twelve whom He also named apostles.*

Luke 6:12, 13

$\mathcal{S}$tay on the right course.
Some day you will be able to look back
on your life's work with satisfaction.

*I have fought the good fight, I have finished the race,
I have kept the faith.*
2 TIMOTHY 4:7

*E*ffective managers know
how to delegate. Pick trustworthy
subordinates, and let them do their job.

*Moreover you shall select from all the people able
men, such as fear God, men of truth, hating covetousness;
and place such over them to be rulers of thousands, rulers
of hundreds, rulers of fifties, and rulers of tens.*

EXODUS 18:21

$\mathcal{M}$ake God the chairman of
the board and senior partner
in your business.

*But Gideon said to them, "I will not rule over
you, nor shall my son rule over you;
the LORD shall rule over you."*
JUDGES 8:23

*P*ower can corrupt.
As we rise, we must be
vigilant lest we fall.

*But when he was strong his heart was
lifted up, to his destruction, . . .*
2 CHRONICLES 26:16

$\mathcal{G}$ood intentions are not
enough. We must make sure we
have communicated them clearly and
that they are understood.

*For he supposed that his brethren would have
understood that God would deliver them by his hand,
but they did not understand.*
ACTS 7:25

$\mathcal{C}$haracter is revealed in
the little things—who you are when
no one is watching.

*He who is faithful in what is least is faithful
also in much; and he who is unjust in what is least
is unjust also in much.*
LUKE 16:10

$\mathcal{L}$ife is a marathon, not a sprint.
It requires self-discipline
and endurance.

*Let us lay aside every weight, and the sin which
so easily ensnares us, and let us run with endurance
the race that is set before us.*
HEBREWS 12:1

$\mathcal{T}$he secret of handling stress
is to release it. Remember, Jesus wants
to carry your burdens.

❏

Casting all your care upon Him,
for He cares for you.
1 PETER 5:7

$\mathscr{T}$hose we choose as our
associates will have an impact on
our values—for good or evil.

*Do not be deceived: Evil company
corrupts good habits.*
1 CORINTHIANS 15:33

$\mathcal{W}$hether we succeed or
fail from the world's point of view,
God uses every circumstance to further
His plans for our lives.

*All things work together for good to
those who love God, to those who are the called
according to His purpose.*
ROMANS 8:28

$\mathcal{B}$efore you appoint a position,
do a thorough background check and,
if possible, observe performance.

■

Do not lay hands on anyone hastily . . .
1 TIMOTHY 5:22

$\mathcal{H}$ard work is indispensable
to financial success—or any other
kind of success.

He who has a slack hand becomes
poor, but the hand of the diligent makes rich.
PROVERBS 10:4

$\mathcal{W}$ait until a strategic moment
to share your plans and ideas. Premature
disclosure could cost you everything.

*Then I arose in the night, I and a few men
with me; I told no one what my God had put in
my heart to do at Jerusalem.*
NEHEMIAH 2:12

$\mathcal{Y}$ou don't start a business venture without proper planning—and you don't follow Christ without a wholehearted commitment.

▪

For which of you, intending to build a tower, does not sit down first and count the cost, whether he has enough to finish it— . . .

LUKE 14:28

$\mathcal{W}$hat God places in our
hands he means for us to enjoy.
But our confidence should be in the
giver, not the gift.

■

*Command those who are rich in this present age
not to be haughty, nor to trust in uncertain riches but in
the living God, who gives us richly all things to enjoy.*
1 TIMOTHY 6:17

$\mathcal{I}$f anyone has a reason
to keep on keeping on, the believer
does. Everything we do for God
counts for eternity.

■

Therefore, my beloved brethren, be steadfast,
immovable, always abounding in the work of the Lord,
knowing that your labor is not in vain in the Lord.
1 CORINTHIANS 15:58

$\mathscr{N}$either wealth nor power lasts forever. Success must be measured by other things.

For riches are not forever, nor does a crown endure to all generations.
PROVERBS 27:24

$\mathcal{E}$xtravagant love means
giving our best in service to God—
in everything we do.

*Then Mary took a pound of very costly oil
of spikenard, anointed the feet of Jesus, and wiped His
feet with her hair. And the house was filled with
the fragrance of the oil.*
JOHN 12:3

*W*ithout organization and leadership, people wander like sheep without a shepherd.

In those days there was no king in Israel;
everyone did what was right in his own eyes.
JUDGES 21:25

*G*od wants us to be
satisfied with what we *have*,
though not with what we *are*.

Now godliness with contentment is great gain.
1 TIMOTHY 6:6

$\mathcal{S}$ome people can
talk a good game, but it is
performance that counts.

Most men will proclaim each his own goodness,
but who can find a faithful man?
PROVERBS 20:6

$\mathcal{B}$elievers are already winners—they have God on their side.

What then shall we say to these things?
If God is for us, who can be against us?
ROMANS 8:31

$\mathcal{T}$he giver gets a double blessing:
the joy of giving and gratitude from
the one receiving.

It is more blessed to give than to receive.
ACTS 20:35

$\mathcal{B}$e a *can* do,
not a *can't* do, person.

◾

*Do all things without complaining
and disputing, . . .*
PHILIPPIANS 2:14

$\mathcal{A}$ Christian should never feel like a victim, but always like a victor.

But thanks be to God, who gives us the victory through our Lord Jesus Christ.
1 CORINTHIANS 15:57

$\mathcal{W}$e buy trouble when we let
greed control us. Money should be
our servant, not our master.

▪

For the love of money is a root of all kinds
of evil, for which some have strayed from the faith in
their greediness, and pierced themselves
through with many sorrows.
1 TIMOTHY 6:10

$\mathcal{I}$f you want to be given
trust, prove yourself trustworthy.

*And if you have not been faithful in
what is another man's, who will give
you what is your own?*
LUKE 16:12

*I*nstead of wasting our lives pursuing what we think will make us happy, we should concentrate on the things that money can't buy—the things God gives us freely.

Why do you spend money for what is not bread, and your wages for what does not satisfy?
ISAIAH 55:2

$\mathscr{H}$onesty is not only the
best policy, it is the will of God.

*Diverse weights are an abomination to
the LORD, and dishonest scales are not good.*
PROVERBS 20:23

*O*ne secret of success is
to know your own weaknesses.
An even greater secret is to know the
One who is the source of your strength.

*My grace is sufficient for you, for
My strength is made perfect in weakness.*
2 CORINTHIANS 12:9

$\mathcal{D}$on't worry about titles
or recognition. Let your accomplishments
speak for themselves.

*Nor did we seek glory from men,
either from you or from others, when we
might have made demands.*
1 THESSALONIANS 2:6

$\mathcal{I}$f your words are uplifting,
people's hearts will be touched
and their lives enriched.

*Let no corrupt word proceed out of your
mouth, but what is good for necessary edification,
that it may impart grace to the hearers.*
EPHESIANS 4:29

$\mathcal{T}$he Bible contains all the principles of success. May we be wise enough to learn them and apply them.

This Book of the Law shall not depart from your mouth, but you shall meditate in it day and night, that you may observe to do according to all that is written in it.

JOSHUA 1:8

$\mathcal{T}$ake it from Solomon,
who had more of it than anyone:
Money doesn't satisfy, nor the things
that money can buy.

He who loves silver will not be satisfied
with silver; nor he who loves abundance,
with increase. This also is vanity.
ECCLESIASTES 5:10

$\mathcal{C}$hrist gives us inner strength
to handle both prosperity and adversity.

*I can do all things through Christ
who strengthens me.*
PHILIPPIANS 4:13

$\mathscr{C}$hristians can rejoice
in the middle of trouble because
they have learned from experience
that God is faithful.

And not only that, but we also glory
in tribulations, knowing that tribulation produces
perseverance; and perseverance, character;
and character, hope.
ROMANS 5:3, 4

$\mathcal{B}$elievers face the same
pressures as unbelievers, but they face
them with faith instead of fear.

*Watch, stand fast in the faith,
be brave, be strong.*
1 CORINTHIANS 16:13

$\mathcal{T}$hose who work for us
know whether we are looking out for
their best interests or our own.

▪

For I have no one like-minded, who will
sincerely care for your state. For all seek their own,
not the things which are of Christ Jesus.
PHILIPPIANS 2:20, 21

$\mathcal{W}$e should provide for
our families, but not covet wealth.
By providing, we may sacrifice for our
families; by coveting, we may end
up sacrificing our families.

*But those who desire to be rich fall into temptation
and a snare, and into many foolish and harmful lusts which
drown men in destruction and perdition.*

1 TIMOTHY 6:9

In the race of the Christian
life, we are responsible to help
each other cross the finish line. God
wants all of us to succeed.

∎

Till we all come to the unity of the faith
and of the knowledge of the Son of God, to a perfect man,
to the measure of the stature of the fullness of Christ.
EPHESIANS 4:13

$\mathcal{T}$he successful person spends time on things that matter, things that make a difference.

And this I pray, that your love may abound still more and more in knowledge and all discernment, that you may approve the things that are excellent, that you may be sincere and without offense till the day of Christ.
PHILIPPIANS 1:9, 10

$\mathcal{G}$od is more interested in the
shape of your character than in the
size of your bank account.

■

*Better is a little with righteousness, than vast
revenues without justice.*
PROVERBS 16:8

$\mathscr{I}$t is foolish to reject criticism.
In order to improve, we need to know
what needs improving.

He who disdains instruction despises his own soul,
but he who heeds rebuke get understanding.
PROVERBS 15:32

$\mathcal{B}$elievers have a major advantage in life—they can turn to God for wisdom and help.

If any of you lacks wisdom, let him ask of God,
who gives to all liberally and without reproach,
and it will be given to him.

JAMES 1:5

$\mathcal{G}$od established the first
workfare program: People need a
hand up, not a handout.

For even when we were with you,
we commanded you this: If anyone will not
work, neither shall he eat.
2 THESSALONIANS 3:10

$\mathcal{G}$od not only supplies all
of our needs, he gives us extra so we
can meet the needs of others.

And God is able to make all grace abound
toward you, that you, always having all sufficiency
in all things, may have an abundance
for every good work.
2 CORINTHIANS 9:8

$\mathcal{T}$o be successful,
we must neither underestimate
nor overestimate our own abilities.

For I say, . . . to everyone who is among you,
not to think of himself more highly
than he ought to think.
ROMANS 12:3

*Y*ou've got just one life
to live for God. Seize the day—
and make the most of it.

*I must work the works of Him who
sent Me while it is day; the night is coming
when no one can work.*
JOHN 9:4

God is pleased when we
use our money wisely and have
something to pass on to our heirs.

*A good man leaves an inheritance to his
children's children, but the wealth of the sinner is
stored up for the righteous.*
PROVERBS 13:22

$\mathcal{O}$ur work is not simply
a means of livelihood, it is part of
our witness to the world.

*That you also aspire to lead a quiet life,
to mind your own business, and to work with
your own hands, as we commanded you.*
1 THESSALONIANS 4:11

$\mathscr{I}$n the end, all rewards
come from God. In his economy,
rewards are directly related
to faithfulness.

*The LORD repay your work, and a full reward be
given you by the LORD God of Israel, under whose
wings you have come for refuge.*
RUTH 2:12

$\mathscr{T}$ruly great people are always humble—like Jesus.

For whoever exalts himself will be humbled, and he who humbles himself will be exalted.

LUKE 14:11

$\mathscr{I}$f you show genuine
concern for your employees and
publicly recognize their accomplishments,
you will reap the rewards of loyalty
and affection.

*Be kindly affectionate to one another with
brotherly love, in honor giving
preference to one another.*
ROMANS 12:10

$\mathscr{C}$hristians to whom
God has entrusted wealth are his
stewards—they must do as much good
as possible with his money.

■

*Command those who are rich in this
present age not to be haughty, nor to trust in
uncertain riches but in the living God, who gives us
richly all things to enjoy.*
1 Timothy 6:17, 18

$\mathscr{T}$hose who work for us deserve
an honest day's pay for an
honest day's work.

Masters, give your bondservants what is
just and fair, knowing that you also
have a Master in heaven.

COLOSSIANS 4:1

$\mathcal{O}$ur co-workers are a gift
from God. We should value them
and treat them as such.

■

I Myself have taken your brethren the Levites
from among the children of Israel; they are a gift
to you, given by the LORD, to do the work
of the tabernacle of meeting.
NUMBERS 18:6

$\mathcal{T}$he Word of God is our
chart and compass. Without it,
we lose our way.

❖

Where there is no revelation,
the people cast off restraint; . . .
PROVERBS 29:18

$\mathcal{S}$uccessful communication
is simply speaking the truth in love.

Let your speech always be with grace,
seasoned with salt, that you may know how
you ought to answer each one.
COLOSSIANS 4:6

Your employees deserve respect—they are made in the image of God.

▪

Receive him forever, no longer as a slave but more than a slave—a beloved brother, especially to me but how much more to you, both in the flesh and in the Lord.

PHILEMON 1:15, 16

*C*hristian employees
are loyal to their employer as a
consequence of being loyal
to their Savior.

*Exhort bondservants to be obedient to their own
masters, to be well pleasing in all things.*
Titus 2:9

*T*he greatest danger of worldly success is self-sufficiency—it so easily masks spiritual poverty.

*Because you say, "I am rich, have become
wealthy, and have need of nothing"—and do not know that
you are wretched, miserable, poor, blind, and naked.*
REVELATION 3:17

$\mathcal{G}$od's requirements for success are straightforward: Keep his commandments, and stay on his path.

▪

You shall walk in all the ways which the LORD your God has commanded you, that you may live and that it may be well with you.
DEUTERONOMY 5:33

*I*f we know Jesus Christ,
we have all the power we need to
pursue personal and spiritual excellence.

*As His divine power has given to us all things
that pertain to life and godliness, through the
knowledge of Him who called us
by glory and virtue, . . .*
2 PETER 1:3

*W*hatever you achieve,
give God the honor and glory.

To God our Savior, who alone is wise,
be glory and majesty, dominion and power,
both now and forever. Amen.
JUDE 25

*I*f material success were
enjoyed in proportion to spiritual
success, how rich would you be?

*Beloved, I pray that you may prosper
in all things and be in health, just
as your soul prospers.*
3 JOHN 2

In God's eyes, success as a
wife and mother, or as a husband
and father, is far more important
than success in a career.

Her children rise up and call her blessed;
her husband also, and he praises her.
PROVERBS 31:28

$\mathcal{W}$hy turn anywhere for
help in time of need except to God?
He is ready and able to help.

■

For the eyes of the LORD run to and fro
throughout the whole earth, to show Himself strong
on behalf of those whose heart is loyal to Him.
2 CHRONICLES 16:9

$\mathcal{I}$f you live by the golden rule,
you are bound to do the
right and fair thing.

Therefore, whatever you want men to do to you,
do also to them, for this is the Law and the Prophets.
MATTHEW 7:12

$\mathcal{D}$on't be afraid to try new things,
even if someone says, "We've never
done it that way before."

And no one puts new wine into old wineskins;
or else the new wine will burst the wineskins and be spilled,
and the wineskins will be ruined. But new wine must be
put into new wineskins, and both are preserved.
PROVERBS 5:37, 38

$\mathcal{P}$eople more readily follow
leaders who roll up their sleeves and
set the pace than those who issue orders
from an armchair.

Shepherd the flock of God which is among you, . . .
not as being lords over those entrusted to you, but
being examples to the flock.
1 PETER 5:2, 3

*C*ommit the matter to God
in prayer, and then take action.

*Nevertheless we made our prayer to our
God and because of them we set a watch against
them day and night.*

NEHEMIAH 4:9

$\mathcal{D}$avid did not look at the size of the obstacle, but at the power of his God.

The LORD, who delivered me from the paw of the lion and from the paw of the bear, He will deliver me from the hand of this Philistine.
1 SAMUEL 17:37

$\mathscr{T}$he wisdom and energy
to acquire wealth come from God.
We must give him glory and take
little for ourselves.

◼

*You shall remember the LORD your God,
for it is He who give you power to get wealth.*
DEUTERONOMY 8:18

$\mathcal{T}$here is nothing so powerful
as an idea whose time has come.

*To everything there is a season,
a time for every purpose under heaven.*
ECCLESIASTES 3:1

*U*ltimately, no one succeeds
in this world without following
God's principles.

*Riches and honor are with me,
enduring riches and righteousness.*
PROVERBS 8:18